D0582114

FOR THE BEST DAD IN THE WORLD

summersdale

FOR THE BEST DAD IN THE WORLD

Summersdale Publishers Ltd
46 West Street
Chichester
West Sussex
PO19 1RP
UK

www.summersdale.com

Printed and bound in the Czech Republic

ISBN: 978-1-84953-567-0

Substantial discounts on bulk quantities of Summersdale books are available to corporations, professional associations and other organisations. For details contact Nicky Douglas by telephone: +44 (0) 1243 756902, fax: +44 (0) 1243 786300 or email: nicky@summersdale.com.

TO...

FROM...

A FATHER IS A GIANT
FROM WHOSE SHOULDERS
YOU CAN SEE FOREVER.

Perry Garfinkel

BLESSED INDEED IS THE
MAN WHO HEARS MANY
GENTLE VOICES CALL
HIM FATHER!

Lydia Maria Child

THERE'S NO PILLOW
QUITE SO SOFT AS A
FATHER'S STRONG
SHOULDER.

Richard L. Evans

I LOVE MY FATHER
AS THE STARS — HE'S
A BRIGHT SHINING
EXAMPLE AND A HAPPY
TWINKLING IN MY HEART.

Anonymous

I CAN ALWAYS
TURN TO YOU

TO HER THE NAME OF
FATHER WAS ANOTHER
NAME FOR LOVE.

Fanny Fern

ONE FATHER IS MORE THAN A HUNDRED SCHOOLMASTERS.

George Herbert

CHARACTER IS
LARGELY CAUGHT, AND
THE FATHER AND THE
HOME SHOULD BE THE
GREAT SOURCES OF
CHARACTER INFECTION.

Frank H. Cheley

A TRULY RICH MAN IS
ONE WHOSE CHILDREN
RUN INTO HIS ARMS
WHEN HIS HANDS
ARE EMPTY.

Anonymous

WHAT DO I OWE MY FATHER? EVERYTHING.

Henry van Dyke

HE OPENED THE JAR OF
PICKLES WHEN NO ONE
ELSE COULD.

Erma Bombeck

MY FATHER GAVE ME
THE GREATEST GIFT
ANYONE COULD GIVE
ANOTHER PERSON: HE
BELIEVED IN ME.

Jim Valvano

YOUR DAD IS THE MAN
WHO DOES ALL THE
HEAVY SHOVELLING FOR
YOUR SANDCASTLE, AND
THEN TELLS YOU YOU'VE
DONE A WONDERFUL JOB.

Anonymous

YOU KNOW
HOW TO MAKE
ME LAUGH

HE DIDN'T TELL ME HOW TO LIVE; HE LIVED, AND LET ME WATCH HIM DO IT.

Clarence Budington Kelland

FATHERHOOD IS
PRETENDING THE
PRESENT YOU LOVE MOST
IS SOAP ON A ROPE.

Bill Cosby

IT IS NOT FLESH AND
BLOOD BUT THE HEART
WHICH MAKES US
FATHERS AND SONS.

Friedrich Schiller

WHEN I WAS A BOY OF
14, MY FATHER WAS
SO IGNORANT I COULD
HARDLY STAND TO HAVE
THE OLD MAN AROUND.
BUT WHEN I GOT TO BE 21,
I WAS ASTONISHED AT HOW
MUCH HE HAD LEARNED
IN SEVEN YEARS.

Mark Twain

YOU MAKE
EVERYTHING
BETTER

ARE WE NOT
LIKE TWO VOLUMES
OF ONE BOOK?

Marceline Desbordes-Valmore

NEVER RAISE YOUR
HAND TO YOUR KIDS. IT
LEAVES YOUR GROIN
UNPROTECTED.

Red Buttons

BY THE TIME A MAN
REALISES THAT MAYBE
HIS FATHER WAS RIGHT,
HE USUALLY HAS A SON
WHO THINKS HE'S WRONG.

Charles Wadsworth

IT IS A WISE FATHER
THAT KNOWS HIS
OWN CHILD.

William Shakespeare

WHEN A FATHER GIVES
TO HIS SON, BOTH
LAUGH; WHEN A SON
GIVES TO HIS FATHER,
BOTH CRY.

Jewish proverb

NO MAN STANDS SO TALL AS WHEN HE STOOPS TO HELP A CHILD.

Abraham Lincoln

MEN LOVE THEIR
CHILDREN, NOT BECAUSE
THEY ARE PROMISING
PLANTS, BUT BECAUSE
THEY ARE THEIRS.

Charles Montagu

NOBLE FATHERS HAVE NOBLE CHILDREN.

Euripides

IF YOUR CHILDREN LOOK
UP TO YOU, YOU'VE MADE
A SUCCESS OF LIFE'S
BIGGEST JOB.

Anonymous

I TALK AND TALK AND
TALK, AND I HAVEN'T
TAUGHT PEOPLE IN 50
YEARS WHAT MY FATHER
TAUGHT BY EXAMPLE IN
ONE WEEK.

Mario Cuomo

FAMILY LIFE IS A BIT
LIKE A RUNNY PEACH
PIE — NOT PERFECT BUT
WHO'S COMPLAINING?

Robert Brault

CHILDREN NEED LOVE, ESPECIALLY WHEN THEY DO NOT DESERVE IT.

Harold S. Hulbert

I LOVED MY FATHER.
I LOOKED FOR HIS
FAITHFUL RESPONSE IN
THE EYES OF MANY MEN.

Patricia Neal

SOMETIMES THE
POOREST MAN LEAVES
HIS CHILDREN THE
RICHEST INHERITANCE.

Ruth E. Renkel

YOU GIVE THE BEST HUGS

ANY MAN CAN BE A
FATHER. IT TAKES
SOMEONE SPECIAL TO
BE A DAD.

Anne Geddes

MY DADDY, HE WAS
SOMEWHERE BETWEEN
GOD AND JOHN WAYNE.

Hank Williams Jr

THE FAMILY IS
ONE OF NATURE'S
MASTERPIECES.

George Santayana

THERE ARE THREE
STAGES OF A MAN'S LIFE:
HE BELIEVES IN SANTA
CLAUS; HE DOESN'T
BELIEVE IN SANTA CLAUS;
HE IS SANTA CLAUS.

Anonymous

YOU'RE MY BEST
FRIEND AS WELL
AS MY DAD

FATHER! TO GOD HIMSELF WE CANNOT GIVE A HOLIER NAME.

William Wordsworth

FAMILY IS THE MOST IMPORTANT THING IN THE WORLD.

Diana, Princess of Wales

IT IS AMAZING HOW
QUICKLY THE KIDS
LEARN TO DRIVE A
CAR, YET ARE UNABLE
TO UNDERSTAND THE
LAWNMOWER.

Ben Bergor

NO MAN I EVER MET WAS
MY FATHER'S EQUAL,
AND I NEVER LOVED ANY
OTHER MAN AS MUCH.

Hedy Lamarr

A DAD IS SOMEONE TO
LOOK UP TO NO MATTER
HOW TALL YOU GROW.

Anonymous

GOVERN A FAMILY
AS YOU WOULD COOK
A SMALL FISH —
VERY GENTLY.

Chinese proverb

YOU KNOW, FATHERS JUST HAVE A WAY OF PUTTING EVERYTHING TOGETHER.

Erika Cosby

BE KIND TO THY
FATHER, FOR WHEN
THOU WERT YOUNG,
WHO LOVED THEE SO
FONDLY AS HE?

Anonymous

A FAMILY IS A PLACE
WHERE PRINCIPLES
ARE HAMMERED AND
HONED ON THE ANVIL OF
EVERYDAY LIVING.

Charles R. Swindoll

LIFE DOESN'T COME
WITH AN INSTRUCTION
BOOK; THAT'S WHY WE
HAVE FATHERS.

H. Jackson Brown Jr

I LOVE YOU
TO THE MOON
AND BACK

FATHERS EMBODY A
DELICIOUS MIXTURE
OF FAMILIARITY AND
NOVELTY. THEY ARE
NOVEL WITHOUT
BEING STRANGE OR
FRIGHTENING.

Louise J. Kaplan

THERE ARE TIMES
WHEN PARENTHOOD
SEEMS NOTHING BUT
FEEDING THE MOUTH
THAT BITES YOU.

Peter De Vries

NOTHING I'VE EVER DONE
HAS GIVEN ME MORE
JOYS AND REWARDS THAN
BEING A FATHER TO
MY CHILDREN.

Bill Cosby

WHEN MY FATHER DIDN'T HAVE MY HAND... HE HAD MY BACK.

Linda Poindexter

I USED TO IMAGINE
ANIMALS RUNNING
UNDER MY BED. I TOLD
MY DAD... HE CUT THE
LEGS OFF THE BED.

Lou Brock

I CANNOT UNDERSTAND
HOW IN THE PAST I
MANAGED TO COPE
WITHOUT GETTING
CUDDLED THIS MANY
TIMES A DAY.

Russell Crowe

NOTHING YOU DO FOR CHILDREN IS EVER WASTED.

Garrison Keillor

A FAMILY IS A
PLACE WHERE MINDS
COME IN CONTACT WITH
ONE ANOTHER.

Buddha

YOU MAKE ME
FEEL SPECIAL
AND LOVED

MY FATHER WAS MY
TEACHER. BUT MOST
IMPORTANTLY HE WAS
A GREAT DAD.

Beau Bridges

TRY, THEREFORE, TO
BE LIKE HIM IN SOME
POINTS, AND YOU WILL
HAVE ACQUIRED A
GREAT DEAL.

Queen Victoria, on her husband,
Prince Albert

THERE IS A SPECIAL
PLACE IN HEAVEN
FOR THE FATHER WHO
TAKES HIS DAUGHTER
SHOPPING.

John Sinor

THE HAND THAT ROCKS
THE CRADLE USUALLY IS
ATTACHED TO SOMEONE
WHO ISN'T GETTING
ENOUGH SLEEP.

John Fiebig

A COMPROMISE IS THE
ART OF DIVIDING A CAKE
IN SUCH A WAY THAT
EVERYONE BELIEVES HE
HAS THE BIGGEST PIECE.

Ludwig Erhard

A GOOD FATHER IS ONE
OF THE MOST UNSUNG,
UNPRAISED... YET ONE
OF THE MOST VALUABLE
ASSETS IN OUR SOCIETY.

Billy Graham

DAD TAUGHT ME
EVERYTHING I KNOW.
UNFORTUNATELY, HE
DIDN'T TEACH ME
EVERYTHING HE KNOWS.

Al Unser Jr

GOOD FATHERS MAKE GOOD SONS.

Anonymous

HOW SWEET 'TIS TO SIT 'NEATH A FOND FATHER'S SMILE.

John Howard Payne

WHAT WE BECOME
DEPENDS ON WHAT OUR
FATHERS TEACH US AT
ODD MOMENTS, WHEN
THEY AREN'T TRYING
TO TEACH US.

Umberto Eco

HE WAS HER GOD,
THE CENTRE OF HER
SMALL WORLD.

Margaret Mitchell

THERE IS MORE TO FATHERS THAN MEETS THE EYE.

Margaret Atwood

YOU ALWAYS SEE THE BEST IN EVERYTHING I DO

THE MOST VALUABLE THING YOU CAN SPEND ON YOUR CHILDREN IS YOUR TIME.

Anonymous

MY BEST TRAINING CAME FROM MY FATHER.

Woodrow Wilson

TO YOU YOUR FATHER
SHOULD BE AS A GOD.

William Shakespeare

OTHER THINGS
MAY CHANGE US, BUT
WE START AND END
WITH FAMILY.

Anthony Brandt

ONLY A FATHER DOESN'T BEGRUDGE HIS SON'S TALENT.

Johann Wolfgang von Goethe

WHY, DAUGHTERS CAN NEVER TAKE TOO MUCH CARE OF THEIR PARENT.

Plautus

CERTAIN IS IT THAT
THERE IS NO KIND OF
AFFECTION SO PURELY
ANGELIC AS OF A FATHER
TO A DAUGHTER.

Joseph Addison

FATHERING IS
NOT SOMETHING
PERFECT MEN DO,
BUT SOMETHING THAT
PERFECTS THE MAN.

Frank Pittman

IT IS MUCH EASIER
TO BECOME A FATHER
THAN TO BE ONE.

Kent Nerburn

CHILDREN LEARN TO SMILE FROM THEIR PARENTS.

Shinichi Suzuki

PARENTHOOD REMAINS
THE GREATEST SINGLE
PRESERVE OF THE
AMATEUR.

Alvin Toffler

A FATHER IS A MAN WHO
CARRIES PHOTOS OF HIS
KIDS WHERE HIS MONEY
USED TO BE.

Anonymous

YOU'RE ALWAYS
LOOKING OUT
FOR ME

NOTHING COULD GET AT
ME IF I CURLED UP ON
MY FATHER'S LAP... ALL
ABOUT HIM WAS SAFE.

Naomi Mitchison

DADS ARE STONE SKIMMERS,
MUD WALLOWERS,
WATER WALLOPERS,
CEILING SWOOPERS,
SHOULDER GALLOPERS,
UPSY-DOWNSY, OVER-AND-
THROUGH, ROUND-AND-
ABOUT WHOOSERS.

Helen Thompson

FOR MANY PEOPLE, GOD IS JUST DAD WITH A MASK ON.

Anonymous

MY DAD IS MY HERO.
I'M NEVER FREE OF
A PROBLEM NOR DO I
TRULY EXPERIENCE A
JOY UNTIL WE SHARE IT.

Nancy Sinatra

I SET THE BAR AT
HALF OF MY DAD. IF I
COULD GET THAT FAR,
I'D CONSIDER MY LIFE
SUCCESSFUL.

Jeb Bush

HAVING ONE CHILD MAKES YOU A PARENT; HAVING TWO YOU ARE A REFEREE.

David Frost

FROM GREAT OAKS
LITTLE ACORNS GROW.

Anonymous

FAMILY IS NOT AN IMPORTANT THING. IT'S EVERYTHING.

Michael J. Fox

NO LOVE IS GREATER
THAN THAT OF A FATHER
FOR HIS SON.

Dan Brown

YOU DON'T CHOOSE YOUR
FAMILY. THEY ARE GOD'S
GIFT TO YOU, AS YOU
ARE TO THEM.

Desmond Tutu

YOU LISTEN
TO ALL MY
STORIES

MY FATHER USED TO SAY
THAT IT'S NEVER TOO
LATE TO DO ANYTHING
YOU WANTED TO DO.

Michael Jordan

HOW PLEASANT IT IS
FOR A FATHER TO SIT
AT HIS CHILD'S BOARD.
IT IS LIKE AN AGED
MAN RECLINING UNDER
THE SHADOW OF AN OAK
WHICH HE HAS PLANTED.

Voltaire

DAD... A SON'S FIRST HERO.

Anonymous

I JUST OWE ALMOST
EVERYTHING TO
MY FATHER.

Margaret Thatcher

MY FATHER HAD A
PROFOUND INFLUENCE
ON ME. HE WAS
A LUNATIC.

Spike Milligan

THE HAPPIEST MOMENTS
OF MY LIFE HAVE BEEN
THE FEW WHICH I HAVE
PASSED AT HOME IN THE
BOSOM OF MY FAMILY.

Thomas Jefferson

YOU TAUGHT
ME SO MUCH

TO US, FAMILY MEANS
PUTTING YOUR ARMS
AROUND EACH OTHER
AND BEING THERE.

Barbara Bush

THE FATHER IS
CONCERNED WITH
PARKING SPACE, THE
CHILDREN WITH OUTER
SPACE, AND THE MOTHER
WITH CLOSET SPACE.

Evan Esar

I LOOKED UP TO MY DAD.
HE WAS ALWAYS ON
A LADDER.

Anonymous

IF YOU MUST HOLD
YOURSELF UP TO YOUR
CHILDREN... HOLD
YOURSELF UP AS A
WARNING AND NOT AS
AN EXAMPLE.

George Bernard Shaw

SETTING TOO GOOD AN
EXAMPLE IS A KIND
OF SLANDER SELDOM
FORGIVEN.

Benjamin Franklin

INFINITE PATIENCE, BOUNDLESS ENTHUSIASM, KINDNESS... AND THE STRENGTH TO SAY 'NO' EVERY NOW AND AGAIN.

Piers Morgan on what it takes
to be a good father

MY MOTHER TAUGHT
ME MY ABCS. FROM MY
FATHER I LEARNED THE
GLORIES OF GOING TO
THE BATHROOM OUTSIDE.

Lewis Grizzard Jr

THE ONLY ROCK I KNOW
THAT STAYS STEADY,
THE ONLY INSTITUTION I
KNOW THAT WORKS,
IS THE FAMILY.

Lee Iacocca

YOU DON'T HAVE
TO DESERVE YOUR
MOTHER'S LOVE. YOU
HAVE TO DESERVE YOUR
FATHER'S. HE'S MORE
PARTICULAR.

Robert Frost

THE BEST INVESTMENT
IS TO GO HOME FROM
WORK EARLY AND
SPEND THE AFTERNOON
THROWING A BALL
AROUND WITH YOUR SON.

Ben Stein

YOU ALWAYS
KNOW HOW TO
FIX THINGS

FAMILIES ARE LIKE FUDGE — MOSTLY SWEET, WITH A FEW NUTS.

Anonymous

ADOLESCENCE BEGINS
WHEN CHILDREN STOP
ASKING QUESTIONS —
BECAUSE THEY KNOW
ALL THE ANSWERS.

Evan Esar

IMAGINATION IS
SOMETHING THAT SITS
UP WITH DAD AND MUM
THE FIRST TIME THEIR
TEENAGER STAYS
OUT LATE.

Lane Olinghouse

A MAN'S CHILDREN
AND HIS GARDEN BOTH
REFLECT THE AMOUNT OF
WEEDING DONE DURING
THE GROWING SEASON.

Anonymous

I DON'T MIND LOOKING INTO THE MIRROR AND SEEING MY FATHER.

Michael Douglas

PARENTS CAN ONLY
ADVISE THEIR CHILDREN
OR POINT THEM IN THE
RIGHT DIRECTION.

Anne Frank

A BABY IS GOD'S OPINION THAT THE WORLD SHOULD GO ON.

Carl Sandburg

JARRELL WAS NOT
SO MUCH A FATHER...
AS AN AFFECTIONATE
ENCYCLOPAEDIA.

Mary Jarrell

YOU ALWAYS
KNOW HOW TO
CHEER ME UP

I HAVE ALWAYS HAD THE
FEELING I COULD DO
ANYTHING AND MY DAD
TOLD ME I COULD.

Ann Richards

BEING A GREAT FATHER
IS LIKE SHAVING. NO
MATTER HOW GOOD YOU
SHAVED TODAY, YOU
HAVE TO DO IT AGAIN
TOMORROW.

Reed Markham

DADS GRAB THEMSELVES
A SPOON AND DIG RIGHT
IN WITH YOU.

Anonymous

HE SEWED BUTTON
EYES ON MY TEDDY BEAR
WHEN ITS OTHER EYES
FELL OFF.

Cynthia Heimel

THE SOONER YOU TREAT YOUR SON AS A MAN, THE SOONER HE WILL BE ONE.

John Dryden

A FATHER'S SOLEMN
DUTY IS TO WATCH
FOOTBALL WITH HIS
CHILDREN AND TEACH
THEM WHEN TO SHOUT
AT THE REF.

Paul Collins

I'M NOT GOING TO HAVE
A BETTER DAY, A MORE
MAGICAL MOMENT, THAN
THE FIRST TIME I HEARD
MY DAUGHTER GIGGLE.

Sean Penn

GETTING A BURP OUT OF YOUR LITTLE THING IS PROBABLY THE GREATEST SATISFACTION I'VE COME ACROSS.

Brad Pitt on his first child

WHEN YOU HAVE
BROUGHT UP KIDS,
THERE ARE MEMORIES
YOU STORE DIRECTLY IN
YOUR TEAR DUCTS.

Robert Brault

PARENTS ARE THE BONES
ON WHICH CHILDREN
SHARPEN THEIR TEETH.

Peter Ustinov

I LOVE PLAYING
GAMES WITH YOU

WE ALL KNEW DAD WAS
THE ONE IN CHARGE:
HE HAD CONTROL OF
THE REMOTE.

Anonymous

ONE'S FAMILY IS
THE MOST IMPORTANT
THING IN LIFE.

Robert Byrd

GIVE A LITTLE LOVE TO
A CHILD, AND YOU GET A
GREAT DEAL BACK.

John Ruskin

ONE OF THE THINGS
THAT BINDS US AS A
FAMILY IS A SHARED
SENSE OF HUMOUR.

Ralph Fiennes

MY MOTHER AND FATHER
WERE BOTH MUCH MORE
REMARKABLE THAN ANY
STORY OF MINE CAN
MAKE THEM.

Orson Welles

I DON'T THINK ANYONE HAS A NORMAL FAMILY.

Edward Furlong

EVEN WHEN FRESHLY
WASHED AND RELIEVED
OF ALL OBVIOUS
CONFECTIONS, CHILDREN
TEND TO BE STICKY.

Fran Lebowitz

LIVE SO THAT WHEN
YOUR CHILDREN THINK
OF FAIRNESS, CARING
AND INTEGRITY, THEY
THINK OF YOU.

H. Jackson Brown Jr

THE MOST IMPORTANT THINGS IN LIFE AREN'T THINGS.

Anthony J. D'Angelo

A CHILD CAN ASK QUESTIONS THAT A WISE MAN CANNOT ANSWER.

Anonymous

YOU TELL THE
BEST JOKES

THE MARK OF A
GOOD PARENT IS THAT
HE CAN HAVE FUN
WHILE BEING ONE.

Marcelene Cox

YOU CAN LEARN MANY
THINGS FROM CHILDREN.
HOW MUCH PATIENCE YOU
HAVE, FOR INSTANCE.

Franklin P. Jones

A ROSE CAN SAY
'I LOVE YOU',
ORCHIDS CAN ENTHRAL,
BUT A WEED BOUQUET IN
A CHUBBY FIST,
YES, THAT SAYS IT ALL.

Anonymous

CLEANING YOUR HOUSE
WHILE YOUR KIDS ARE
STILL GROWING UP IS
LIKE SHOVELLING THE
WALK BEFORE IT
STOPS SNOWING.

Phyllis Diller

ANYONE WHO
THINKS THE ART OF
CONVERSATION IS DEAD
OUGHT TO TELL A CHILD
TO GO TO BED.

Robert Gallagher

THE ONLY THING WORTH STEALING IS A KISS FROM A SLEEPING CHILD.

Joe Houldsworth

LIFE IS NOT MEASURED
BY THE BREATHS WE
TAKE, BUT BY THE
MOMENTS THAT TAKE
OUR BREATH AWAY.

Anonymous

TO LAUGH OFTEN AND MUCH; TO WIN THE RESPECT OF INTELLIGENT PEOPLE AND THE AFFECTION OF CHILDREN... TO KNOW EVEN ONE LIFE HAS BREATHED EASIER BECAUSE YOU HAVE LIVED.

Ralph Waldo Emerson on success

THERE'S SOMETHING
LIKE A LINE OF GOLD
THREAD RUNNING
THROUGH A MAN'S
WORDS WHEN HE TALKS
TO HIS DAUGHTER.

John Gregory Brown

MOTHER WOULD... SAY,
'YOU'RE TEARING UP
THE GRASS.'
'WE'RE NOT RAISING
GRASS,' DAD WOULD REPLY,
'WE'RE RAISING BOYS.'

Harmon Killebrew